Make a Plan, SCOOBY-DOO!™

A Guide to HOME SAFETY

by Steve Korté

PEBBLE
a capstone imprint

Published by Pebble, an imprint of Capstone
1710 Roe Crest Drive, North Mankato, Minnesota 56003
capstonepub.com

Library of Congress Cataloging-in-Publication Data
is available on the Library of Congress website.
ISBN: 9798875220517 (hardcover)
ISBN: 9798875220463 (paperback)
ISBN: 9798875220470 (ebook PDF)

Summary: From smoke detectors going off to too many cords being plugged in, there are a lot of dangers around the house. Scooby-Doo and the Mystery Inc. gang cover important home safety tips.

Image Credits
Getty Images: AJ_Watt, 22, Henrik Sorensen, 4; Shutterstock: Aleksey Mnogosmyslov, 24, Anton Prohorov, 2 (bottom), Drawlab19 (fire icon), 5 and throughout, Drazen Zigic, 10, FabrikaSimf, 27, Garor, 8, Irina Gutyryak, 14, izzuanroslan, 17, klee048, 2 (top), Mr Boiko Oleg, 12 (top), Nuamfolio, 18, Pabrik Creative, 7, paikong, 12 (bottom), pakww, 13, PeopleImages–Yuri A, cover, 9 (right), 25, pics five, 6, Pixel-Shot, 23, Polina Tomtosova (doodles), 1 and throughout, Pressmaster, 26, Prostock-studio, 5, Sheila Say, 20, Sorapop Udomsri, 28, Streamlight Studios, 21, tawanroong, 9 (left), Vivienstock, 16, watercolor 15 (notepad), back cover and throughout

Editorial Credits
Editor: Christianne Jones; Designer: Bobbie Nuytten; Media Researcher: Svetlana Zhurkin; Production Specialist: Katy LaVigne

Printed and bound in China. 6274

The Mystery Inc. team keeps everyone safe in Crystal Cove by chasing away monsters and ghosts. But home safety is more than chasing monsters and ghosts. Home safety is making smart choices and staying alert. When you don't know what to do, just ask Scooby-Doo!

Uh-oh! There is smoke coming from the oven!

Beep! Beep! Beep! Now the smoke detector is going off!

SCOOBY-DOO, what should I do?

You should leave the house and follow your family's Fire Safety Plan. If your family doesn't have one, make one today.

FRED'S FIRE SAFETY PLAN

- If you smell something burning or if your smoke alarm starts beeping, quickly go outside. There is no time to stop for toys or other items.
- Move far away from the building. Pick a place where everyone can meet, like a tree or garage.
- An adult will call 911 to request help.

DON'T FORGET!
An adult should replace the batteries in your smoke detectors every six months. Keep a working fire extinguisher in the kitchen too.
SD

Yum! This new candle smells like cookies and vanilla. There's a lighter sitting by it. I'm not supposed to use matches, but I bet I could use the lighter.

SCOOBY-DOO,
what should I do?

You should leave it alone. Using matches or a lighter can be dangerous. You could burn yourself or start a fire. Give the lighter to an adult to light candles. Then put it in a safe place.

DON'T FORGET!
Never leave a candle burning unattended—even if an adult is home.

I'm hungry! I want to make some toast, but the toaster isn't plugged in. There's no room in the outlet for the toaster plug.

SCOOBY-DOO,
what should I do?

You should unplug an item that isn't being used. Never plug too many items into the same outlet. They could overheat and cause a fire.

VELMA'S ELECTRIC SAFETY RULES

- If an electrical cord is torn or coming apart, don't touch it. It could shock you.
- Never place electrical cords under a rug. They can get too hot and cause a fire.
- Keep liquids away from all electronics. Water and electronics don't mix.
- Do not touch electrical cords, appliances, or outlets with wet hands. They could shock you.
- Never yank a cord to unplug an item. It will damage the cord. Pull it gently by the plug.

We just got a cat, but she isn't very friendly. She keeps hissing at me and showing her teeth, but I really want to cuddle her.

SCOOBY-DOO, what should I do?

You should stay calm and back away slowly. Don't run or scream. And don't try to pick up an angry animal.

DAPHNE'S PET-SMART SAFETY RULES

- Always be gentle with animals. Don't pull their tails or ears.
- Never approach an animal when it is eating, sleeping, chewing on a toy, or caring for its young.
- Don't make loud noises or sudden moves when approaching an animal.
- If you see a dog or cat you don't know, don't run up to it. Stay calm and quiet.
- Always ask an adult if it's okay to pet their animal. Then hold out your hand slowly so it can sniff you first.

Ding-dong! Someone is at the front door, but I'm home alone.

SCOOBY-DOO, what should I do?

Don't answer the door. Keep the door locked and stay out of sight. If an adult is home, have them answer the door.

What is a cute door called?
A-door-able!
!?
KNOCK
KNOCK

I have the coolest project to build, but I need a drill and some other sharp tools. I'm supposed to wait for my mom to help me, but I really want to make it now.

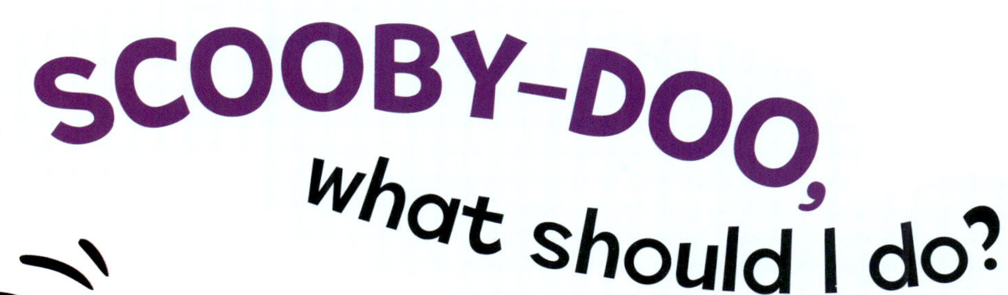
SCOOBY-DOO,
what should I do?

You should wait for an adult to help you. It's always safer—and more fun—to have a building buddy. While you wait, you can organize the project and make sure you have everything ready.

DON'T FORGET!
Safely put away tools after a project. Be sure to clean up your work area too.

Now you can be safe and sound at home. Just remember to follow a few simple and SAFE rules.

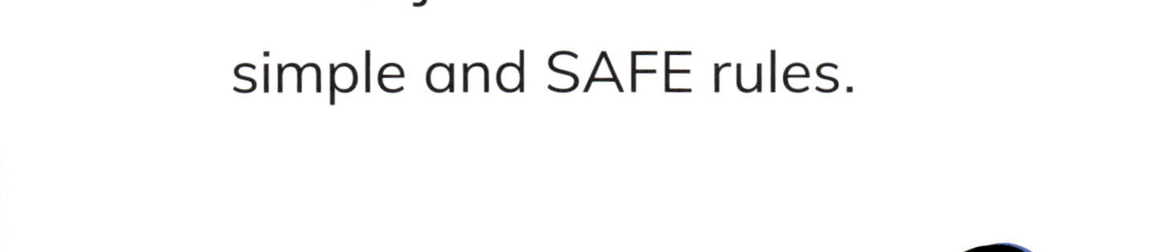

Stay away from danger.

Ask an adult for help.

Follow instructions from an adult.

Emergencies—make a plan.

It looks like we've got ourselves a safety plan, gang!
Like, safety is groovy, man!
Scooby-dooby-doo!

Scooby-Doo's Home Safety Review

1. You see smoke coming from the oven. What should you do?

a. take a nap

b. open the oven

c. go outside

2. How often should you replace the batteries in your smoke detectors?

a. every 3 months

b. every 6 months

c. once a year

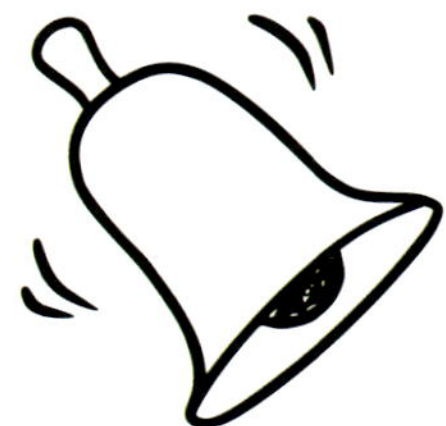

3. If you find matches or a lighter, what should you do?

a. use them

b. sell them

c. give them to an adult

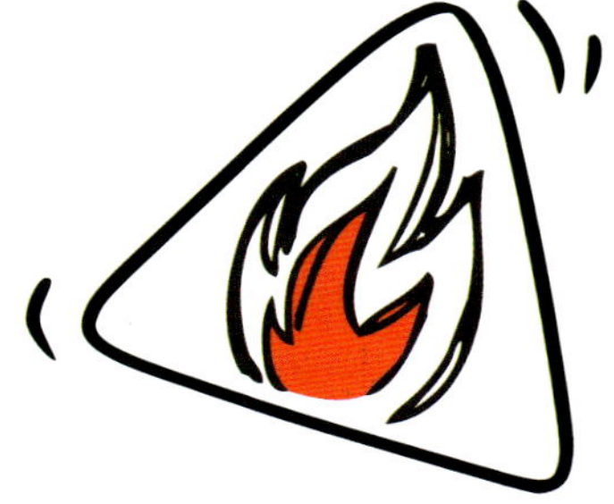

4. Which one of these actions should be part of your family's fire safety plan?

a. meet at a set location

b. grab your favorite toys

c. take time leaving

5. What is one safety rule for electrical cords?

a. Put them under rugs.

b. Plug lots of them into one outlet.

c. Replace a cord that is torn or frayed.

6. How should you act around animals?

a. overly excited and loud

b. calm and quiet

c. angry and rude

7. The doorbell rings, but you are home alone. What should you do?

a. open the door

b. wave from a window

c. don't answer the door

8. What can you do while waiting for an adult to help build a project?

a. play with the drill

b. organize your project pieces

c. sharpen tools

ANSWERS: 1. c 2. b 3. c 4. a 5. c 6. b 7. c 8. b

How many signs can YOU find?

There are different warning signs throughout this book. See how many of each you can find!

About the Author

Steve Korté is the author of more than 100 books, featuring characters as diverse as Batman, Bigfoot, and the Loch Ness Monster. As a former editor at DC Comics, he worked on hundreds of titles, including *75 Years of DC Comics*, *Wonder Woman: The Complete History*, and *Jack Cole and Plastic Man*. He lives in New York City with his husband Bill.